by JOYCE CAROL OATES

Novels
With Shuddering Fall (1964)
A Garden of Earthly Delights (1967)
Expensive People (1968)
Them (1969)
Wonderland (1971)
Do With Me What You Will (1973)

Stories
By the North Gate (1963)
Upon the Sweeping Flood (1966)
The Wheel of Love (1970)
Marriages and Infidelities (1972)
The Hungry Ghosts (1974)

Poetry
Women In Love (1968)
Anonymous Sins (1969)
Love and Its Derangements (1970)
Angel Fire (1973)
Dreaming America (1973)

Drama
Miracle Play (1974)

Criticism
The Edge of Impossibility (1972)
The Hostile Sun: the Poetry of D. H. Lawrence (1973)

Editor
Scenes From American Life (1973)

Joyce Carol Oates

MIRACLE PLAY

LOS ANGELES
BLACK SPARROW PRESS
1974

LIBRARY OF CONGRESS CATALOGING IN PUBLICATION DATA

Oates, Joyce Carol, 1938-
  Miracle play.

    A play.
    I. Title.
PS3565.A8M5   812'.5'4   74-19270
ISBN 0-87685-215-0 (de luxe)
ISBN 0-87685-214-2 (lib. bdg.)
ISBN 0-87685-213-4 (pbk.)

for Daniel Freudenberger

MIRACLE PLAY was first presented by the New Phoenix
Repertory Company at the Playhouse II Theatre, 359 West 48
Street, New York City, on December 30, 1973. Scenery,
projections and lighting were designed by James Tilton and
Daniel Freudenberger directed. The cast was as follows:

Beatie Roscoe. . . . . Marcella Lowery

Titus Skinner. . . . . Robert Guillaume

Mason Skinner. . . . . Ernest Thomas

Earl Roscoe. . . . . Donny Burks

Rollie. . . . . Ralph Wilcox

Bob Skinner. . . . . Jaison Walker

Mrs. Skinner. . . . . Louise Stubbs

Prosecutor. . . . . John Benson

Kidd. . . . . F. Murray Abraham

Conroy Roscoe. . . . . David Connell

Production Stage Manager: Ellen Barry

Production photographs by James Tilton

Illustrations (following page 68)

NOTE:

The play moves in and out of three dimensions: the "natural" in which characters speak exactly as the people they represent speak; the "farcical" in which characters speak exactly as a strange audience might suppose them to speak, parodying both themselves and the audience; and the "mystical" in which characters speak not as their stage selves, or as the selves they represent would speak, but as essences, as pure souls, not defined by color or age or personality of any kind.

It should not move freely back and forth through these dimensions, however; one should sense the transition, almost a painfulness, a strain, a nearly muscular resistance. The audience should sense how clumsily and horribly the three dimensions come together.

CHARACTERS:

Beatie Roscoe, age 16
Conroy Roscoe, age 31
Earl Roscoe, age 19

Titus Skinner, age 29
Mason Skinner, age 23
Mrs. Skinner, age 50
Bob Skinner, age 14

Rollie, age 20
Kidd, age 35 (a white man)
Prosecutor, age 35 (a white man)

Miracle Play

SCENE 1

An ordinary room, with an unmade bed, a bureau with drawers partly opened, clothing and towels lying about, a closet door standing open. It is a naturalistic scene. The door opens and BEATIE enters, pushed through the doorway by TITUS.

BEATIE is wearing a yellow dress. TITUS is wearing a stylish suit, with a shirt of some expensive silkish material; no necktie. Throughout the play TITUS exhibits a certain self-consciousness, a nervous but intelligent awareness of himself, as if he is continually anticipating his own words and actions, and anticipating their effect upon others. From time to time he shows an awareness of the audience.

BEATIE

Howcome you marched me up here?

(She is nervous, but tries to appear angry.)

What's this? This crap? This bed an' stuff, all this layin' around, you lookin' for maid-service? This ain't room service. You grabbed hold of the wrong girl.

TITUS

Just preparing a scene for a little talk. This room rings a doorbell with you . . . ? No accidental room, huh? You know all this, huh?

(He takes her by the shoulders and forces her to look around.)

BEATIE

(trying to squirm away from him)

That hurts—

TITUS

(pretending surprise)

Oh hurts? What hurts? What's that word—*hurts*? That an important word in your vocabulary, honey? You want to spell out that word for me?

BEATIE

I don't need to stand for this—

TITUS

Look, honey, you seen how easy it is to kidnap a cute little fox like you from right down in the street, all kinds of people hangin' around, them girl friends of yours never gave no alarm did they? You got a strong-souled boy friend, honey, to snatch you right up off the sidewalk an' march you up here, back to the scene of the crime, and a little interrogation. Now, honey, now look: I'm goin' to put a direct question to you; what did you do with that stuff?

BEATIE

(guiltily)

What stuff?

TITUS

Five hundred dollars of it, Beatie, honey, you sneaked away with five hundred dollars of my trade, which is invested in me by sources that don't stand for no displeasure—all this is not news, right? My surprise is how dumb you are, sneakin' out like that. Night comes, dawn comes, people open their eyes an' wake up, people don't take no night-time shit from other people when the night is over—right? What did you do with it?

BEATIE

With what? With what? I don't know what the hell—

(*TITUS stands patiently, mockingly, watching her. She walks around the room, as if trying to distract him; out of the corner of her eye she sees the door to the corridor. Very subtly, TITUS dissuades her from trying to run for the door, by moving only an inch or so; he stands with his arms folded. He is very much in control of the scene.*)

BEATIE

I am no stranger to all of this crap, this smelly junk an' shit an' garbage you lay down in—I don't put no claim to it, either, to clean it up or make that stinkin' bed—maybe one time I would trip all over the stairs, just to put away Titus Skinner's drawers, maybe one time, yes, but I learned a certain lesson—I don't plan to be no second-time loser with you—I—I know how taken-up Titus is with his plans—

(*She pauses, goes to the bed, as if to make it up. Her manner is bright, innocent.*)

Can't stand to see all this mess— Long's I'm up here I might's well—

TITUS

(*ironically*)

No use, Beatie. Nope. No use. You got none of the right magic to undo harm. You just a moron-brained little girl, you don't have a hint of your best advantage. Let that stuff alone.

BEATIE

(*pretending not to understand*)

This is such a surprise place, judgin' from how you walk around

17

outside—you an' them outfits—I'm surprised you don't rent no special maid service to tend to you—

(*TITUS tears the bedclothes away from her. He throws them down in a heap. BEATIE backs away from him.*)

TITUS

You got it hid somewhere, for a joke? Blackmail joke? Or what is it? You plannin' on usin' that stuff yourself, you graduated that far along? Or you goin' to sell it on the street, handfuls at a time? Where is it hid, honey? Time is runnin' short. You know I am a busy man.

BEATIE

I don't know what—I don't know— I— You talkin' about something I should know? Something missin' from this room? Look Titus,

(*laughing*)

I am just too confused for thought—my brain is flooded with things pictures looks like flashes of dirty bedclothes—or butterfly wings—or—

TITUS

Where is it hid? I hope to Jesus you got it hid well, Beatie, because I am countin' on retrievin' that stuff in fifteen minutes—today is a Friday and my Fridays are busy schedules— Where'd you put it? You never brought it home to your momma's place, I rule that out right away, your momma ain't goin' to lay back an' close her eyes, *she* got to get her nose in everything! So where did you hide it, honey?

BEATIE

Hide what?

TITUS

You want your face ripped?

BEATIE

Ripped how come?

TITUS

Oh, Jesus, you can't get through this scene, you just a damn sad moron-brained little girl, you can't utter no lie to Titus, why, Jesus, Titus is a boy friend to you a hundred times over—you an' all them girls like you—Titus asks the questions an' determines the truth of the statement— If you can't lie better than how you doin', honey, you ought not to trespass the law. This room is my private place, an' the merchandise I got here, when I got it, is my private trade, an' you got to be much wiser than Titus to violate his territory. Now, honey, you know all this an' I believe you only sneaked out with some bagful of stuff for a trick, because you is a cute little girl, right?—you planned in your head a surprise for you' nigger, how pleased he goin' to be when you tell him it was a joke—that it? A joke? But now the joke lost its touch, honey. This is Friday pay-day an' check-day, as you know, an' no day for a discussion. Beatie, you better tell me before I get over-excited an' out of hand—*where* you got it hid?

BEATIE

I never took nothin' from you—I never— I wasn't— I don't—

(*TITUS seizes her by the arm and shakes her. BEATIE breaks away.*)

BEATIE

You're crazy like a wild man—you're all out of focus—

TITUS

You stole somethin' from me an' I want it back!

BEATIE

You big damn bull—

TITUS

(*becoming angrier*)

Didn't lose it, did you? Didn't trade it off, did you? Howcome you look so scared? You got instincts in your legs, girl, don't you? But I got my own instincts too. You want a workin'-over, is that

19

so? Want some emergency-ward-work done on your face, do you? I goin' to unstitch you an' they goin' to stitch you up again—big needles an' thick black thread stitchin' you' face up again when I finish— Where you headed?

(*BEATIE runs to the window, as if to throw herself out. TITUS grabs her.*)

BEATIE

(*terrified*)

This-here high up—out the window it's high up— How'd I get up here, third or fourth floor of some place—?

TITUS

You want to see how high up? You want to experience how high up?

(*holding her in front of the window*)

Beatie, I never allowed for this long a discussion, I comin' to the end of my patience . . . .

(*pause*)

You *got* that stuff, ain't you? Didn't give it away, did you?

(*pause*)

Beatie, honey, you didn't give it away, did you . . . ?

BEATIE

I never . . . I don't know what . . . I don't know what you mean . . . .

TITUS

Jesus, did you give it away . . . ? To Conroy? Did you give it away to Conroy?

BEATIE

(beginning to cry, but girlish, "innocent")

I am so mixed-up this morning . . . I am not myself . . . . What's
this about Conroy? I stay clean away from Conroy . . . .

TITUS

Was he behind it? Was he?

BEATIE

Conroy don't know my business—

TITUS

Yes, you always been close to Conroy, all of your family close
together—your big-mouth momma tryin' to say she ain't
ashamed of Conroy—puttin' him up, pretendin' to my momma's
face he is equal to *me*— Why, Conroy on the short list! Conroy
scheduled for disaster! *He* put you to stealin' that stuff, didn't
he?—*he* plannin' on a vacation all his own, usin' it up day by
day, five hundred dollars of a investment of *Titus's*—

BEATIE

I don't do no favors for Conroy, Conroy just a sick mess—

TITUS

You goin' to be a sickern Conroy if that stuff is gone—if he is
hidin' out with it— You better be able to put your finger on
where that motherfucker is hidin' or—

*(BEATIE struggles with him and he shakes her
violently.)*

You want manhandlin'! Damn drug-out little running-sore bitch
you' momma is ashamed of— Don't you try goin' sideways, you
ain't disappearing into no magic. *I* handle the magic here—
Where is Conroy? Did you give it to him? Where is he? You want
me to track him down in person?

(becoming angrier)

Bitch! I am boxed into a situation where my connections are watchin' every move close—they got their eye on me—I don't have nobody laugh at me, up an' down the street people waitin' to laugh at me, they scared as hell face-to-face but they waitin' for me to misstep an' turn my back— You are tantalizin' me close to murder! Time I get finished with you, the doctor students goin' to have a real party-time matching up parts of you' face, down there at the morgue—you know how they do down there?—they drug the bodies out of the river or pick 'em up on the street an' lay 'em out on a table, an' perform the autopsy, white kids, studying to be doctors— Why Beatie, honey, they gonna pull stuff out of you' insides hand over hand

(*He makes a comic, cruel gesture.*)

an' stand around laughin' like hell—

BEATIE

(*screaming*)

I never stole nothin'! Nothin' from you!

TITUS

Where is it? Where—

(*suddenly calm*)

I gon' punish you in style.

(*He throws her down onto the bed, and rips open the back of her dress. He picks up a metal coat hanger from the floor and raises it to strike her back.*)

BEATIE

(*screaming*)

Titus— Titus—

SCENE 2

An unfurnished room, with a few crates, cartons,
unidentified piles of things pushed back against the
wall; what appears to be a mattress, with a single
blanket loosely on it, and a few kitchenware items: a
hot-plate, plugged in; some silverware, cups, etc. on
the floor. The door opens and MASON SKINNER is
pushed into the room, blindfolded, by EARL
ROSCOE and his friend ROLLIE. ROLLIE is
carrying a package of sugar, in a recognizable carton.

MASON

(speaking rapidly)

I don't know nothin' about Titus! I ain't connected to him! First
thing I heard about, about how he went after Beatie, first thing I
heard I run into the house an' told my momma, an' I said to her
Jesus Christ! Now you see how crazy he has got! Earl? I know
that's you there, Earl—I know it's you—Earl?

(EARL does not answer. He forces MASON to his
knees, and points to the hot-plate, a pot that is lying on
the floor, and gestures that ROLLIE should go out
somewhere and fill the pot with water. ROLLIE nods
and does this.)

MASON

(in a voice that moves from sincere protestation
through a kind of farcical whine to terror)

23

Earl? Earl? Howcome you goin' after me? I got nothin' to do with Titus! Nothin'! He don't never turn up at the place, he sends some cash along sometimes an' bought Momma a coat—an' a rug—but Jesus, Jesus, you know I ain't in with him, he don't think shit of me—Earl, you know that, you know that! Earl? Why you doin' this? Is this a kidnapping, is it to get Titus to come around? Because—because—he ain't never goin' to give a damn about me—

(*ROLLIE returns with a pot of water, which is set on the hot-plate. EARL opens the package of sugar and shakes it near MASON'S face; then he seizes MASON'S head and puts a pinch of sugar to his lips.*)

MASON

What's that? What? . . . sugar? What you goin' to do with sugar?

(*wildly*)

You boilin' some water there? Is that sugar-water? What you want to do that for, Earl, you don't plan on hurtin' me, do you? I ain't no enemy of yours—I ain't even a real brother to Titus, I am his half-brother—Titus always push me around, Titus is no *brother* to me. Earl? Howcome you so mean, now, you turned mean overnight? I never did no harm to you—you ask Beatie if I ain't always been nice to her—an' Beatie likes me O.K., Beatie don't know about this, does she?—Beatie? She would scream for you to stop if—

(*MASON tries to get to his feet, but they push him down to his knees again. EARL ties his hands behind him.*)

MASON

(*trying to be calm, then frightened, then terrified, then calm again*)

Titus don't give shit for me! He's no close brother to me or none of us! He breakin' my momma's heart!—Earl, I saw it was you—*I saw it was you*—an' Rollie, is that Rollie? I known who it was! Now this got to be a joke to scare me—because there is no connection between Titus Skinner an' me or anybody else— He

24

only goin' to laugh if you mess me up. He only goin' to *laugh*. He make fun of me all the time an' laugh at where I work, he got it in his head I am a garbage man, an' he don't let go of that, which is a lie—I am on the truck for Parks an' Recreation—an' we got rakes an' things—an' it mostly ain't garbage but just leaves an' stuff from the trees—in the park—an' run-down squirrels, shit like that, mashed things an' squashed-up, or a dog, you know, a dog if somebody run over him an' we get the call—an'—an' it ain't no garbage truck—an' Titus just laugh at me for it, he ain't no connection to me, an' it not goin' to break his heart if—if—if you—

(*pause*)

You ain't sincerely boilin' some water—? You ain't goin' to blame me for Beatie hurt like that, are you—? I don't know Titus's business, I don't know where he is right at this moment or any other given moment—Earl, you listen! Titus is no brother to me, no close brother—he a bastard got to cause trouble—that ain't no paid-for car of his—he not makin' nowhere like four thousand a week, like the talk has it, up an' down the street—that a lot of bullshit talk—who goin' to hand him that much money? I ask you that—? Up at the top they makin' that kind of money but Titus ain't at the top—he is a liar—what he says—he is just goin' to laugh— Earl, why ain't you talkin',to me? This is a joke to scare me? You want me to say where Titus gone, where he hidin' out—? I don't know nothin' about Titus, not one fact, not one address anywhere in this city or anywhere else—you want me to telephone him, or—? . . . The last time I run into him, on the street where I was walkin', an' he just drove on by in his car an' give me a nod—I think he gave me a nod—had on sunglasses like mirrors—I couldn't see where he was lookin'—I hear the talk, like you—I hear lots of wild talk— I don't know nothin' about Titus an' his life! He kicked free of all of us! He kickin' free of his old self! He ain't my close tie an' he ain't my brother—he ain't nothin' to do with me— Only goin' to laugh like hell an' say, *How come you boys messed up Mason's ugly face, already messed-up bad enough!* . . . You ain't goin' to dump no water on me, Earl?—how am I connected to you?—howcome you got me here, right here, kneelin' here, what am I to you an' what Titus got to do with me—or you—or anybody that is human—?

25

SCENE 3

The SKINNER living room. There are many items of furniture, including a shabby sofa.

BOB is alone. The door opens and MRS. SKINNER leads MASON in. He is bandaged.

MASON sits on the sofa to the left, very carefully. MRS. SKINNER hurries over to him and helps him lie down.

BOB

You been out there a long time—you an' Momma—I was worried—uh—

MRS. S

(angrily to BOB)

Turn on that television!

BOB

(after a long pause)

Titus got to know about this . . . Titus got to be informed . . . .

MASON

No.

BOB

I'm gonna get Titus onto this . . . gonna get him over here . . . .

MASON

No!

BOB

You just afraid of more hurt . . . . But . . . .

(gathering strength)

But I ain't afraid of it, I ain't, I'm gonna notify Titus on all of this—

MRS. S

Shut your mouth. Titus ain't in town, Titus gone.

BOB

He out of town on business but he comin' back— You know *for sure* Titus comin' back—

MASON

No—no more—they'll kill me—

MRS. S

(to BOB)

Now you see you got him all worked up, you shootin' that mouth of yours— Mason been through a lot, honey, you got to sympathize. Mason been down at the clinic an' you know how long he was waitin'? He was waitin' a whole day long, an' he very worn-out now, an' not himself.

(to MASON)

Now you just lay still. You goin' to be fine now, you lay still an' rest. All goin' to get healed. They said come back an' get the bandage changed an' some ointment an' stuff an' we gon' do all

that when the time comes, goin' to get you back to yourself
again—

MASON

(*suddenly afraid*)

No—they'll kill me—

MRS. S

Honey, they ain't nowhere near. Ain't goin' to get you. Honey,
lay still, you shiverin' an' better lay still—

(*She tries to put a blanket over him. He thrusts it away.
Then, when she draws it up over him again, he
acquiesces.*)

In a minute you goin' be all set in place an' you can watch the
show comin' on. How's that? You goin' to lay still an' rest up an'
get back to yourself an' there is no hurry about nothin'—lots of
shows comin' up every day—

BOB

(*to MRS. S*)

Did they fix up his face?

(*MRS. SKINNER makes a gesture to silence him.*)

MASON

I hear some noise—

MRS. S

That's the television show. You don't need to look at it, honey, if
your eyes waterin', you just lay there an' listen an' relax an' let
them pills work on you.

MASON

There is something out there—some noise—I can hear them
messin' around—

BOB

Howcome he talks so funny?

MRS. S

Your brother is tryin' to concentrate on that show an' you shut up!

(*grabbing BOB and walking him to the other side of the room*)

Look, Mason is hurt bad, he is miserable with pain an' you got to imagine it, for yourself, an' not be so damn smart. Did anybody telephone here? Did Titus call?

BOB

Telephone . . . ? No, nobody . . . . You think Titus goin' to call?

MRS. S

That phone not workin' right anyway, if he wanted to call. Nobody called?

BOB

It never rung . . . . Maybe it don't work.

MRS. S

Beatie's momma hangin' around on the street down there, she so drunk she can't stand up. An' Beatie swingin' her ass up an' down the street, nobody never begged Beatie to run after my Titus, an' Jesus!—she must have been exploded out of her mind to steal from him!— Who the hell gon' steal from my Titus an' survive?

BOB

How is Beatie?

MRS. S

Well, I heard she ain't too bad—ain't ripped up in the face—I don't know, the way the talk goes up an' down the street, what the hell should you believe?— He broke some ribs an' some other stuff an' she bein' treated at Receiving an' her momma don't need to act this is the first time Beatie Roscoe got herself kicked hard by some man. That girl, that girl when she *eleven years old* been in trouble, nobody better try to blame any of this on Titus—

BOB

(*impatiently*)

Momma, what did you tell the police about this?

MRS. S

What police? No police hung around, no police was after me.

BOB

Didn't the doctors say nothin'?—about Mason?

MRS. S

I don't know, I don't know if it was a doctor come by or not—that place too big an' mixed-up—somebody came on by an' was in a hurry to fix Mason up an' I told him it was a accident, some hot water spilled out in the kitchen, or something like that, an' the man don't ask no questions about it because he got work to do. I don't interfere with them, they on their own an' I on my own. Mason, he quiet all the time. *He* real brave. He was sayin' to me, *Momma, don't tell the police or Titus either, please Momma, please—*

BOB

(*contemptuously*)

He is really crazy, thinkin' Titus won't know about this!

MRS. S

(*sympathetically*)

Now you right, honey, you right, you *very* right, but . . . but we don't want to agitate Mason right now . . . . He's got it in his head to be afraid of them all. Earl an' Rollie that did it to him,

31

but also the police, and also his own brother . . . he all mixed-up, but I ain't got the heart to tell him. Titus, now, Titus ain't no angel, I am not claiming that . . . got a worse temper than his father did . . . but

(*becoming proud*)

. . . but one thing you got to say, Titus is his own self, he is into the economy an' makin' that economy *work*—he is not hangin' around on the street or shootin' needles in himself—Clara Roscoe, now, she been on welfare the last ten years an' got no shame, an' her girl Beatie is just a whore, an' her son Conroy, why Conroy aged a old man, aged fifty years the last time I seen him—he very *sick* with drugs an' no kind of pride—an' her boy Earl, why Earl is goin' to be—

BOB

Momma, you did so good not tellin' the police anything— Momma, that was so sharp— If Titus come home an' found that out, that you went to the police an' not to him—why—Titus be heartbroke—

SCENE 4

A storage room. TITUS, dressed as in Scene 1, is standing with one foot on EARL, who lies on his side with his hands bound together. ROLLIE is on the floor nearby, sitting awkwardly; his hands are also bound. Both boys are dressed shabbily and there are bloodstains on the front of EARL'S shirt. Slide: TRACEY and MORRIS, TITUS'S friends, looming in the background.

TITUS

(in a lordly, musical, farcical voice)

You scared boys, ain't you? Scared? Scared as hell? Ain't you? Got a real purpose to bein' scared, you bring Titus Skinner back from a high-level deal three hundred miles away . . . Only good luck for you boys I am in a party mood from some handsome negotiations. Earl Roscoe, you, you look up when I talk. Ain't you in a frenzy, now?

(prods EARL, who holds himself rigid)

you just puttin'-on to be brave. I know. I know niggers like you inside an' out. I known your slut sister Beatie inside an' out the first time I got within a yard of her, an' your drunk momma ain't much improvement, an' your brother Conroy rotting on his feet—been on his bad sick habit far before *my* time in the trade—Ain't my connection, none of it, I just laugh at it. I just laugh. Earl, boy, you payin' close attention to me . . . ? You respecting my words . . .?

33

(EARL *manages to look up at* TITUS. *This immedi-*
ately pleases him; he withdraws his foot and squats
down between EARL *and* ROLLIE.)

TITUS

(*seriously, more "naturally"*)

How she comin' along, boy?

EARL

She okay.

TITUS

Took to a doctor, or what?

EARL

. . . down to the hospital . . . they been fixin' her up . . . got some
stuff . . . some tape on her . . .

TITUS

What, broke ribs?

(EARL, *sullenly, does not reply.* TITUS *pauses, as if*
contemplating something.)

TITUS

I maybe gon' pay the bills; I got connections with some real
doctor, what they call a *internist* . . . . That a real doctor, that
you never seen around here, a real expensive doctor you can't
just contact walkin' in off the street . . . lots of them in the city if
you know how to find them.

(*laughs*)

There is lots of surprisin' things, boy, all over the city, lots of
things niggers like you never get hold of . . . . That ain't the first
time you' sister got worked over, was it?

EARL

You never had no right—

ROLLIE

(*to EARL, desperately*)

Shut up!

TITUS

Look, *her* face better off than my brother Mason's, ain't it?

EARL

We don't know nothin' about that—

TITUS

Nothin' about what?

EARL

Somethin' said to happen to you' brother, we heard the talk all over, we never—

TITUS

I hear the news a long distance away. I ain't even got time to check it. I act very fast, you got to be impressed how fast I check back here. But I come back to one surprise: that you two boys is still in town.

ROLLIE

We don't know nothin' about Mason—

EARL

No, I only got the news from—

TITUS

No, no, you handlin' you'selves bad as Beatie, you boys *can't lie* worth a damn.

*(laughs, straightens and becomes more musical
again in his speech)*

Serve you right, you boys, somebody come along an' fix up you'
handsome faces like my brother's—that got to be a sight, a
spectacle— Howcome you gone after Mason? Mason ain't no
significance. Howcome you never tried for me myself? . . . Oh,
you is enjoyin' such luck that Titus Skinner is in a party mood,
made some top-drawer connections on the map! *Not no map you
ever seen!* Damn if anybody on that map ever heard about
Beatie or Mason or any such shit, not nothin', points out to you
how much it matters— It don't matter, it don't matter what
happen down here in this neighborhood, it don't matter one shit,
you got that? *It don't matter.* Ain't nobody interested. The man
call me in an' I think to myself, *Titus, he gon' write you off the
list!* But he never heard or gave no goddam about Beatie nor any
of my personal business, he got high plans for me instead, he told
me, *Titus, got high plans for you, been shiftin' an' arrangin'
personnel, an' we ready for some promotion upward anytime
you ready* . . . . You understandin' any of this?

EARL

(cautiously)

Howcome you drug us in here—?

TITUS

Howcome you think?

EARL

You think we did somethin' to Mason an'—

TITUS

But you innocent, huh? You both innocent?

EARL

Yeah, we innocent—

TITUS

(*laughing*)

You victims of a severe miscalculation, you think I give one damn about Mason—*Mason Skinner*—he ain't my brother, not that half-ass. He ain't *nothin'*. I don't contend my mind with him.

(*makes a contemptuous gesture*)

Look, I on the business-scale. I playin' the open market—you know what that is? Open market? Economy market? You understand words like that?

(*EARL and ROLLIE appear baffled.*)

This minute, you is all lookin' at a individual headed for the future! I goin' to soar upward with the spiral, ain't nothin' to stop me! All of life an' stuff you boys never heard of is goin' up, it's growin' up, upward, you follow that? It's a bulgin' to make things grow, like plants comin'—uh—carrots an' trees—things down in the ground, that insist on their way *up*. That natural. That the *natural law*. A whole place—a city—a nation—is constructed similar—it goes up—the fast-thinkin' boys is like trees themselves an' they break loose an' go up with it an' they is saved—

(*TITUS pauses, as if a little embarrassed by his mysticism, then squats down again beside EARL and seizes his hair.*)

Hey, you is a familiar face, you, boy, you is a smart little motherfucker, ain't you? You is just the size of all them smart little niggers applyin' for jobs with me, with Titus Skinner. You is, you is just the size! You tell me one fact, Earl: did you' big-mouth momma call the police on me?

EARL

No—

TITUS

Didn't call no police?

EARL

No, she never—

TITUS

That a wise, important fact.

(*nods*)

Yes, boy, that a miracle-fact for you . . . When you get back to you' momma, you instruct her she did right, an' you' Beatie the same. Some of them police hangin' on me too close. . . . Hey, you, Earl, hey, hey . . . . Is you sorry you messed up Mason's ugly face?

EARL

I never—

TITUS

Look, he only a half-brother! He don't count!

(*laughs*)

Howcome you boys messed up Mason's ugly face, messed-up bad enough before!

(*seriously*)

I don't trust Mason. He got the sad, sad heart, he always lookin' at me an' thinkin' some thought I can't get to. He nothin' but a garbage man but he got this . . . this . . .

(*vaguely*)

He got this look to his face, only now he ain't got no face, the news I heard, no face left . . . All that a very strange business, very complicated to think about . . .

38

(TITUS breaks out of this spell and walks around energetically.)

Now look, I gon' pronounce sentence on you boys. I like one of them judges downtown. I calculatin' all the odds an' back-an'-forth an' come to this thought: two husky boys makin' a mistake, what's the crime to society of that mistake? Got to weigh it all. On one hand I got to deal punishment, on the other hand I got to calculate. But, you know how the street is—all up an' down the street they watchin', they lookin' to see what Titus gon' do now. Howcome you' sweet sister got her ass broke—I got a reputation most precarious to maintain—You' brother Conroy got hands on certain merchandise of mine an' he ain't anywhere in town an' I got my main interest in him— Where's Conroy hidin'?

EARL

I got no connection with Conroy—

TITUS

Where is he?

EARL

Jesus, Conroy might be dead—I don't know—I got no connection—

ROLLIE

Conroy ain't been seen—

TITUS

You think he is gone, he is out of town for good?

EARL

—got no connection with Conroy—

TITUS

You boys thought you was a television show, draggin' my half-ass brother away like that. Look here.

39

(takes a coin out of his pocket)

I gon' give you a lesson in floatin' currency. Like: a coin is worth fifty cents, but it is also worth nothin'. It ain't nothin', no nourishment. It ain't nothin', but it's worth fifty cents . . . . That's my reputation. I come up the difficult way, I did my grubbin' an' never laid back, *I* not a welfare shithead like the rest of you niggers, an' I ain't no garbage man neither, nor anything classifiable on the records

(proudly)

when them records is goin' to be written up . . . . So, boys, I gon' put a proposition to you.

> *(TITUS'S manner is clever, cruel, a self-consciousness so total as to be almost mystic, egoless, as if he were the author not only of his own words but of the entire scene.)*

This coin here is you' Fate. You believe in Fate? O.K. I gon' toss this coin in the prescribed manner an' give you heads-or-tails choice of it, an' no trick to it, for I am above common trickery. You call it heads an' if it is heads, why, why I gon' release you an' shake hands eye-to-eye, that my privilege, to raise up two black boys that is good promisin' material . . . . That my privilege an' my power in life, when I stand lookin' down at the shit laid all over this city that is *you*. But, but now, but on the other hand, now, there is a fact of life not so easy, that don't have the happy endin' like on television, that you boys is got to realize and that fact of life is makin' a mistake when you call the coin. Like, like you name it *heads* an' it turn out *tails*. That must be taken in stride. You got that? So you boys make the wrong mistake an' you in the hands of Fate an' cryin' out for corrective procedure.

> *(He unscrews the cap on a can of kerosene.)*

Hey, Jesus, this-here stuff *strong*! This goes right up into you' head an' clears it out! This-here good stuff, Grade-A guaranteed stuff, no questions asked, no money-back. Earl, honey, what your opinion on this—?

(He holds the can so that EARL can smell it; EARL, terrified, says nothing.)

You, Rollie? You just a sad-faced nigger, ain't you? You just not assimilatin' all this, ain't you?

(holds it for ROLLIE to smell)

Now, here is the deal: the punishment gon' be Chinese style, how they do over there. You seen them pictures in the paper—? —the monks or whatever they are, how they burn them up? They step out of line one inch an' they is *burned* up, no questions asked, that the rule of the law over there, them, uh, Buddhists or whatever they is . . . I forget which one does the thing, which side is which, but it *effective* in the public eye, an' points out how nobody don't need to take no shit from nobody, which is my philosophy also. I got a better style than dumpin' some hot water on a poor bastard's head, you got to admit.

(like an impresario, or a magician)

So. I gon' toss my coin, that I have faith in. You, boys,

(to slide of TRACEY and MORRIS)

you stand right up close to be impartial witnesses, there is *no* trickery involved in Titus Skinner, I gon' be fair like the Statue of Liberty itself holdin' the scales both ways, no prejudice. Now you don't let down you' momma an' the other folks waitin' for you, this is a important moment in you' life, beginnin' a whole new career with Titus Skinner or gettin' burnt up alive in two minutes . . . . Boy, you remember one thing: there is a universal lesson here, an' it don't matter which way you choose, you learnt the lesson inside-out . . . . You ready?

(He tosses the coin, it rolls on the floor, he steps on it and stands waiting.)

41

SCENE 5

A darkened stage, which slowly lights up to reveal BEATIE, seated on a folding chair, and the PROSE-CUTOR, a white man, who is standing.

PROSECUTOR

Beatie, I'm sorry to keep this up, I wish I could let you go home . . . but I think you know that justice has got to be done now. You realize it, don't you? You can't protect murderers like Titus Skinner any longer. You've got to recognize that these murderers are killing *you* . . . killing your kind . . . I mean your families, your brothers. It isn't a question of protecting innocent people. Beatie? Miss Roscoe? Will you answer my questions?

BEATIE

(in a daze)

It was all this commotion down on the street . . . an' I got Momma out of bed . . . it was, oh, it was maybe four in the mornin' . . . an' I heard the noises . . . they was people makin' noise . . . .

PROSECUTOR

It was 4:25 A.M.

BEATIE

An' my God I put on some clothes an' run down there . . . I see my friend Lana goin' down ahead of me an' I called out, I asked her what it was, an' she said she don't know, she was goin' down

43

just in her pajamas . . . .

(*laughs*)

Lana is real wild, she a crazy one, but close to my heart . . . she my own age by two weeks . . . . So I run down front with her an' these people yellin' out on the sidewalk, an' we got there, an' these two . . . .

(*pauses*)

These two boys . . . bodies . . . . There was these . . . . People was runnin' up from all over an' sayin', *Look here!* an' I could smell how it was somethin' burnt like meat . . . an' Lana an' me got there, an' there was these . . . these two . . . .

(*She falls silent. The PROSECUTOR is very sympathetic.*)

BEATIE

Well . . . they was all burned . . . . It was both of them, they was all burned . . . . Out on the sidewalk front of our place. Somebody asked Momma, *Where you' boy, Earl—he up in bed or what?* Somebody said, *That look like Earl, that one.* They was arguin' about it. Then I got mixed-up an' had to be put somewhere . . . . I no longer got a stable constitution; I gettin' bad as Momma.

(*laughing*)

Momma not herself all the time. She come round, she apologize how wild she been actin', down here, actin' so crazy an' tryin' to kick an' bite you . . . . She don't mean no harm but is gone off her head. When I was beat-up she took good care of me, she cried an' said, she said this was exactly what she expect, from me tailin' around Titus Skinner. But she didn't go wild with it, because I was not hurt bad . . . an' he never messed up my face . . . . She took good care of me, she a very loving mother when it necessary. But . . . But with Earl . . . . With Earl it kind of pointless . . . . It kind of pointless . . . to be a loving mother . . . or anything else . . . . You could not tell Earl from Rollie, that

44

was a confusion. Some white man was askin' me to identify my brother, an' he laid stress on the clothes aspect of it, like shoes that was left, but Jesus

(*in amazement*)

they was alike . . . . So if you wanted to grieve for one you would grieve for the other . . . . I get mixed-up. Like a face . . . a face is what tells us apart, ain't it?

(*She looks at the PROSECUTOR, who nods with compassion but does not answer her question.*)

I mean a face . . . on the outside, here . . . a face is the way you tell people apart, an' people who ain't you? It is the method, ain't it?

(*She leans around in her chair to appeal to unseen others.*)

What the difference between us, if there ain't no face left?

(*wildly*)

Oh I gon' get more mixed-up, raked around in my brains . . . like my poor Momma . . . . I gon' get sick if somebody don't spell out some answers to me . . . .

(*after a pause, more calmly*)

Well they got no face left, that's a fact. Somebody took pictures of them. But none for the newspaper up close, it was too nasty, they don't print the pictures like that. They take them, though.

(*vaguely*)

All goin' into the record . . . into the book . . . .

(*The PROSECUTOR leafs through his notes, carefully.*)

PROSECUTOR

This all began, Beatie, when you took several hundred dollars' worth of narcotics from Titus Skinner's room?

BEATIE

(*vaguely*)

. . . It's bein' writ down, somebody takin' notes an' recordin' it . . . The answers to the questions right there, no mix-up to it . . . .

PROSECUTOR

Beatie . . . ? Can you answer my question, please? This all began when you stole five hundred dollars' worth of heroin from Titus Skinner's room on 119th Street, is that an accurate representation of the truth? Or would you like to modify it?

BEATIE

Earl always a loud boy, but nice to me . . . Since he ten, eleven, a real little kid he stayin' away from where we lived . . . . I don't know that Rollie real well. But he was bad company for Earl, them two boys bad on each other . . . too soft-flexible . . . takin' stuff, runnin' around the street high-up . . . . Momma give up on him long time ago like she give up on Conroy . . . .

PROSECUTOR

Your brother, Conroy, asked you to steal the narcotics, didn't he? That's what we've heard, from reliable sources. Where is Conroy?

BEATIE

The evil eye put it to me . . . lookin' at me . . . . Conroy, he so sick an' messy, his arms all shrunk-up . . . got the evil eye inside him, in his head an' lookin' out. I was feelin' so good. I was feelin' high-up myself, the way Titus made a fuss around me an' bought me some stuff . . . bought me a coat an' some boots . . . . A fur coat . . . . The boots was white leather an' made by hand, cost seventy-five dollars from Saks . . . . I got mixed-up in my own mind, how far I could go with Titus. He was actin' so foolish over me that I . . . . I made a mistake . . . Conroy put the thought to me, to take some package or somethin' that wouldn't be noticed, just some package, a bag of somethin', when Titus had a lot of it, an' maybe wouldn't notice . . . . Conroy so sick, he so crazy off his head . . . . So I mishandled some item from . . . .

(*pause*)

a problematical person.

PROSECUTOR

At which point Titus Skinner beat you up. Right? And then your brother and a friend of his tortured Mason Skinner, is that correct? And Titus Skinner, to retaliate, kidnapped and murdered your brother and his friend. Yes, we know all this, it's clear and predictable.

(*He looks around.*)

We were able to predict, almost to the hour, when the bodies would be found . . . .

BEATIE

. . . Long time before the commotion out front, all that night I been havin' these off-an'-on dreams . . . bad dreams . . . . I felt very electric. I known Earl was up to somethin', that was the talk. Then later I got the news on Mason Skinner. So I known it all. I was just waitin'. Downtown they give me some pills, so I could sleep, but anyway I was wakin' up an' my mouth tasted so rotten . . . . I felt all jumpy like with electric sparks. Momma, she was so drunk, laid down with all her clothes on an' snored right off, but I more sensitive an' was put to the torture, them dreams I had. I think there is too much electric power loose in a city this size. If people bein' careless take the plugs out of the sockets on the wall, why, it stands to reason . . . it stands to logical reason . . . that electricity would get loose an' into the air . . . . An' you multiply that by millions people an' you see what a thing it is . . . . One time there was a story in the Sunday paper on the electric chair, that they used to use here in state, but decided against, an' there was pictures of it, an' I showed a picture of it to Earl—he was maybe fifteen then—an' I said to Earl, *So you ain't gon' wind up in this chair after all!* They got it

47

in a museum or somethin' now. So Earl said, *No, I got to leave this state for that privilege.* I didn't get these words. But, but later I did, I think I did, later other things come to help me, an' I half-known what he meant. Like, like you are out walkin' on the street in open daylight an' you think to you'self, all at once: *What if I run out in front of that bus?* I have seen a shadow self of Beatie Roscoe do such a thing. I know. Earl had the electric in him, all jumps an' sparks. Couldn't make use of it. They said him an' Rollie did some hard thing to Mason Skinner, an' maybe so, maybe not, I never checked out the information. But if so it was the electricity done it, jumpin' out of Earl, to turn him so nervous an' mean like he been the last few years . . . . He worse than Conroy, even. Conroy always been mean but not out-of-the-way mean, if you wasn't in his way, he not goin' to run over you. Earl different, Earl too excitable. There is a lesson in it . . . but I don't know what it is.

PROSECUTOR

Beatie . . . ? You'll testify for us, won't you? You'll be a witness against him?

BEATIE

Who? Against who?

PROSECUTOR

You know who. *Titus Skinner.*

BEATIE

Which one that . . . ? Look here.

(*She stands, opens the top of her dress, so that the welts on her back can be seen.*)

An' around back here on my head . . . there is awful aches an' seizures, from where he pounded me on the floor. Used up every pimp trick he known, on me, beatin' me where it don't show, for protection of the product . . . . It's a razor-edge, how mad they get . . . a man when he starts beatin' on you . . . unless his mind's in perfect poise, like Titus's, he could go too far an' mash the face in.

PROSECUTOR

You need only tell us the truth, and stick to your story, and we'll protect you and your mother and your brother, we'll take every precaution . . . . Beatie, you've agreed?

BEATIE

Wish I hadn't been so sick, so bad-feelin', I could maybe gone over to Mason Skinner's an' talked to him . . . him an' me, we got along O.K., he a nice guy, he not like the other Skinners that they would spit in you' eye if they could . . . . Oh Jesus, if it'd been Mason Skinner instead of Titus, that I got so high on . . . . I got to see that man face-to-face an' make a sense of all this. You put Titus Skinner away, it don't matter, he got control of things an' make life miserable for people. They all scared of him, don't like him but they scared of him, like worship him, they don't want to get killed like my brother . . . . All this is complex behavior. I ain't equipped to deal with it. But somebody got to deal with it . . .

(*vaguely*)

. . . got to make a sense of it an' get it reduced to a word you can understand . . . .

PROSECUTOR

Is that word going to be *yes* . . . ?

(*waits patiently, while BEATIE shakes her head slowly, as if not understanding him*)

Yes, Beatie, is it *yes* . . . ? We'll protect you and your family. We know exactly how to handle this. Titus Skinner is a marked man —we've got warrants out for him and we'll get him in a few hours! He's been arrested eight times and he's always gotten away, he's squirmed out of assault charges, nighttime theft charges, possession of narcotics charges, but this time it's first-degree homicide. That bastard was making four thousand a week, I happen to know! *Four thousand a week!* . . . You can help us out, Beatie, Titus Skinner was your lover for a period of six to eight weeks, and you are well-informed about him. We'll be extremely grateful to you. What do you say?

49

BEATIE

(uncertainly)

Somebody was my *lover* . . . ? Somebody loved me . . . ? When was that . . . ?

PROSECUTOR

Are you going to testify on our side? Are you going to cooperate?

BEATIE

What was that you said, what word . . . ? You said . . . ?

PROSECUTOR

We'll keep you and your family in custody, Beatie, in protective custody out of town, in another city . . . . *Are you going to cooperate?*

BEATIE

. . . Too late by now anyway, he put his mark on me. Not on my face but everywhere else. I used up. I all used up. Sixteen years old goin' on nothin' . . . .

PROSECUTOR

(turns off recorder)

That means *yes*, then. I assume that means *yes*.

BEATIE

Might as well be . . . . Yes. Yes, I will testify. Yes. I used up anyhow, might as well keep goin'. *Yes.*

PROSECUTOR

(perfunctory now)

And we'll protect you, Beatie. You'll be absolutely safe until the trial and during the trial, and we promise a conviction . . . . We're going to stop this kind of lawlessness and make this city safe for everyone, regardless of color or race.

SCENE 6

KIDD, the white defense attorney, an attractive man in his mid-thirties, is pacing and speaking excitedly before the JUDGE, an older white man whose image is projected. Off to the left, at a table, sits TITUS, dressed in a cheap, "respectable" suit.

KIDD

(very moved)

. . . Your Honor, for one thing . . . for one thing the police acted without legitimate reason to suspect the men they arrested . . . they were acting out of hatred, ignorant hatred . . . . Your Honor, they got a search warrant on flimsy evidence, I have reason to suspect that they acted solely on the word of a police informer . . . an enemy of Titus Skinner's . . . someone who wants to see Titus in trouble . . . . Your Honor, my client's life has been threatened often in the past, and it was simply for reasons of self-protection that he had the weapons the police seized, in his car . . . and the narcotics they claim to have discovered, in a room rented under the nama of Skinner, Your Honor, Your Honor I submit that the narcotics were *not* the property of any of these men here before you this morning, they claim absolute ignorance of any narcotics whatsoever . . . . Your Honor, I am not accusing the police of having planted this evidence. I am only accusing them . . . I am trying to make you see, Your Honor, make you *see* . . . . Your Honor, if you will look again at the record, you will see that Titus Skinner, aged 29, has *never* been convicted of a serious crime. His earliest arrests were for misdemeanors . . . petty thefts . . . he spent eight months in the detention home, and his probation officer, Mr. Hough, indicated, Your Honor, indicated that Titus was one of the more responsible boys at the Home . . . and that his year of probation was without incident . . . . Your Honor, all this took place twelve years ago, and since then my client has been arrested but *not* convicted of the charges brought against him by the police . . . . Your Honor, I am going to move that all these charges be dropped, since the evidence is patently flimsy and it is an outrage—

JUDGE

(*on tape*)

Motion denied.

KIDD

Your Honor, the charges of first-degree homicide, these charges are without precedent on such transparent evidence—the prosecution is in possession of certain witnesses I insist upon meeting with—I insist upon a meeting with all the witnesses—I insist upon a realization of the horror of this act, this search-and-seize warrant issued from this very room, on make-shift evidence, distortions brought about by racial hatred, deeply-felt unconscious or conscious urges toward genocide—in evidence everywhere in our environment, and I do not exclude the law-enforcement officers of our city, I do not accuse but I do not exclude, the record of the courts, the record of poorly disguised racial bigotry in the form of judicial procedure—I am entering a plea for—

JUDGE

(*on tape*)

Denied.

KIDD

—for a reduction of the charges—

(*As if their timing is off, KIDD glances at the JUDGE, then resumes.*)

52

I am requesting a reduction of the charges from first-degree homicide to manslaughter.

JUDGE

(*on tape*)

Denied.

KIDD

I am requesting bail for my clients, reasonable bail to allow them to return to their families, Your Honor. I request bail for these young men on the basis, Your Honor, that the prosecution has no witnesses for the alleged crime, has put together a shabby and outrageous case, has no real case, is acting out of hostility and not compassion, it is all hearsay, it is simple street gossip, Your Honor, despicable, shameful, vengeful impulses from the gutter . . . . I request, may it please Your Honor, total cognizance of the humanity of these healthy young men, imprisoned beneath ceilings much too low for their height, shackled like dangerous animals, beasts denied their full humanity by a racist society—young men bewildered and terrified *at this very moment* by their surroundings, their isolation, their heritage from the days of slavery, their crowded conditions, their poor schooling, black genes, their ravenous bellies, their anguished starving souls starving for existence—I plead in their behalf—I declare—I insist that they are innocent as we are all innocent, under the law of our nation, we are all innocent until someone somewhere tracks us down and arrests us and proves in open—open—court how we are guilty, and causes to be brought in against us in open court, in absolute openness, by a jury of our peers, causes to be brought in against us, all of us, a verdict of *Guilty* . . . . Your Honor,

(*He speaks passionately, wildly.*)

Your Honor, until that day . . . until that hour . . . we are innocent and my clients are innocent . . . we are all innocent under the law until that verdict is handed down . . . And so, and so . . . and so I . . .

53

(He pauses. After a moment he approaches the bench and speaks more calmly, normally.)

I request that my clients be released on bail.

JUDGE

(on tape)

Denied.

(KIDD considers this. Slide of JUDGE off. KIDD approaches TITUS.)

KIDD

He was touched, he was very moved. I saw it. He was very moved. Did you see it? I saw it. He's up for re-election and has to be cagey, though. But I saw it, I felt it. Didn't you? Didn't you feel it? I'm very confident . . .

TITUS

What happened? What went on? What was all that shit? Somebody more gon' get killed, somebody gon' be annihilated all over this shithead town—I want a change of venue!

(TITUS grabs KIDD and is about to strike him, then stalks out instead.)

I want some new attorney's got some knowledge-about-town, not no preacher crap-head, I want my money back, I'm entering a plea to be my own attorney an' the hell with everybody else—

KIDD

(calling after him, idealistically and yet half-mockingly)

We touched him—we made an impression—justice will be done —don't lose confidence—don't lose faith in America—

SCENE 7

*A bare stage, onto which CONROY ROSCOE walks.
He is shabbily dressed, appears much older than his
real age of thirty-one, and his sense of self—of a
confined ego—is minimal. He is in a state of perpetual
terror, which is interrupted or relieved by half-human
states of awareness, cunning, practicality, even a kind
of humor. (He is not a symbol of anything; he is, or
was, a conscious human being who has been altered
into something both larger and smaller than his specific
"self.")*

CONROY

(peering around, frightened; is aware of the audience)

Where is this? Is this St. Louis? I was headed there . . . I was
meant to go there . . . but if I got here instead I was meant to get
here . . . . They got the police after me, I know the police is
huntin' me down . . . or huntin' somebody down that looks like
me . . . the way I looked . . . I . . . uh . . . But I a sick man, no
threat, I not askin' for mercy but only justice . . . to be let alone
to die . . . to ask of you the patience, the kind patience, to be
given the normal amount of time to die, that in my case the
doctor said was, uh, two-three years he stated, unless something
speeded it up . . . which he also stated . . .

(shakes head in amusement)

Oh Jesus, he a nice young guy, he scaint as hell just to see me, he
shook up, he say to me like in a whisper *You're dying!* I was sick
that day but not so sick to lose my dignity, so I said to him, he

55

was a white kid an' scairt of how I got the shudders, I said *So are you!*—an' it shook him up the more, to notice I had a operatin' brain. But it ain't operatin' to do damage, it ain't operatin' at full-function, don't you hold that against me!—I no harm to you, I not a threat or problem—

(*stares at audience*)

I lookin' in a dark place an' the dark place lookin' back at me. It don't speak. It waitin' for me to make the false move.

(*After a moment he seems to re-assert himself as CONROY.*)

. . . No . . . No, I am Conroy, I am the one, yes, if you lookin' for him, but, the fact is, this is the fact, the fact is I am very sick an' my memory is gone an' it was maybe somebody set down an' argued with me an' said I am named Conroy an' got it drummed an' shouted into my head so I gave in an' said *All right! I'm Conroy!*—so you let me alone an' stop shoutin' at me! That might of happened; last night or some other night. I been loose for a long time. I been on the run for my life . . . . But I known you would catch up to me . . .

(*peers at audience*)

You ain't no friends of Titus . . . ? Titus, he very mean, he very famous-mean, I would not go against Titus, no, not if I was crazy even, never . . . . Titus beyond me. I ain't in his way. I am innocent. I goin' to lay down off to the side not on the sidewalk, an' I ain't in any of you' way, I ain't no trouble to you . . . . Howcome my little brother got himself killed, it ain't part of my curiosity, I too sick, but I believe he made the choice. You can't stop them, the young kids. They is already too wild for my generation, I heard he was burned up by a match, but I don't pay attention to such shit, that just nigger-talk an' speculatin' an' I too sick for it an' so far out of town an' it ain't even clear if I am Conroy or if somebody, some black bastard, talked me into that name an' walked off free himself . . . . All my life I been dedicated to my own explanation, that took me a long time to figure out. I always on the *search*. I searchin' for the famous powder, that you put it into a liquid an' a needle an' into the

blood, an' it make you magic . . . like God . . . . I dedicated to
that search, I very dedicated an' worn out with years of it . . . I
always gettin' news that somebody got the real thing to deal me,
the new formula, an' I got the faith in it, an' always ready, an'
ain't found it yet . . . but when they invent it, I gon' be first
customer, I gon' rush in there no matter how sick I am . . . . Now
I pretty bad, I goin' to pieces fast. I recognize this. But even if I
layin' down in the street half dead when they make the
discovery, even then I gon' jump up an' get in the front of the
line, to get that powder . . . . I am a inflatable deflatable
balloon. I am in the shape of a man, a black man, but it a
balloon in that shape, an' I in charge of blowin' the balloon up,
an' then it leak out the air by itself, slow, until I is flat to nothin'
an' got to start hustlin' again to blow myself up . . . . That a daily
task, in fact a four-times-a-day task. When I was stronger I
could hustle 12-14 hours a day, now I a little sick, but I try for
the full work-day, I dedicated to the problem an' willin' to work
hard every day, that mean *every day*, no Saturday-Sunday off,
or special Monday holiday, no vacation in the summer or
anytime, I don't never rest my ass moren a few hours . . . . But I
ninety years old now in the insides, an' the doctor say my guts is
shrivel up all over, an' that got the solid force of science behind
it, a forecast like that, so, so if you is concerned about *me*

(*laughs*)

you is mistaken . . . because I ain't goin' to harm you or nobody
in you' family . . . . Long as I last, I goin' to be a out-of-the-way
man. I a good customer of people like Titus, I pour money into
the pockets of the economy, I don't ask for money-back, for
guarantee, for repair-work or realignment or recyclin' or nothin'
of that nature, because the product I buy is never open to doubt
. . . If you tryin' to get me back home for the police, why, why I
in no condition to testify, I all confused an' no-good. I am fast
disappearing. I am a dyin' man an' take it in stride . . . I am not
a complainer . . . I am always a good customer an' no
troublemaker whether I am in my own mind or somebody else's
. . . I only plead innocent, I no harm to you, I no threat . . . I am
dyin' of innocence . . . .

SCENE 8

A street in front of the Skinners' house.

MRS. S

Look here

(extends hands)

how I am shakin', I am shakin' in an' out just like this—you know that son of a bitch Herman—

BOB

Momma, what the hell—

MRS. S

You listen! That Herman, that big black son' bitch, he bump into me in the drugstore an' say to me, how Titus goin' be sent up for damn sure this time, an' once he out of the way all the Skinners better haul themselves out of here—

BOB

Herman told you that? *Herman?*

MRS. S

He say lots of people is holdin' back, what they goin' to do—oh, he was drunk an' shootin' off his mouth, but he was tellin' the truth—I am just shakin', I am so nervous of all this— An he tryin' to postpone that trial, that Mr. Kidd, he always tryin' to change things around, the court schedule all mixed-up to high heaven—

BOB

Howcome Herman got it in for us? Titus ain't never—

MRS. S

Not just Herman! They all fed up, they waitin' like cats in the alley for somethin' to be tossed out, somethin' dead, they just gloatin' an' talkin' so free about Titus—now you know they *never*—

BOB

Well, Titus ain't hauled off yet. Titus got a very good chance—

MRS. S

You know they *never* talkin' so free before—in fact they was necessarily on my side, 'gainst Beatie's Momma—they all tellin' me how Titus known how to treat that little bitch—she so stuck-up thinkin' she pretty—now they is all lookin' at me, I'm afraid to go down onto the sidewalk—

BOB

Mason ain't no damn help to you, layin' there like that—Jesus, I so sick of tryin' to hammer some sense in that brain of his . . . He actin' weird all the time . . . . he got a long hatred for Titus, he ain't goin' to admit it to you nor anybody, he just damn don't want Titus to get free.

SCENE 9

MASON

I remember that I went to school! . . . yes, that was me, I think it
was me . . . wasn't that me? Mason Skinner? Back a long time
ago . . . uh . . . he was very small and scared . . . I can see
him . . . I remember . . . he went up front of the room on the
last day of school, all the kids were dressed up an' had their
poems to recite, an' he went up front an' the teacher then—it
was a woman—the teacher said *O.K., now Mason, everybody
quieted down now an' ready*— So he said the poem right off—

> God appears and God is light
> To those poor souls who dwell in night
> But does a human form display
> To those who dwell in realms of day.

He said it right off . . . he didn't make a mistake . . . I think . . .

(pause)

Then I betrayed everybody's confidence, the tax-payers lost faith
in me, or somebody like me, maybe my brother did some bad
things with schoolbooks, that the tax-payers bought an' provided
me with . . . or somebody like me . . . . Which one of them was
it? I got a lot of brothers. Jesus, I got so many of them . . . they
are anxious to lean hard on me . . . dump boiling water over my
head . . . make sure it is sweetened with sugar to make it stick to
the skin an' not run off . . . . Earl Roscoe, who is now dead, did a
thing to my face that woke me up hard: now I am tryin' to get
back to who I am, which one of them. I am maybe Earl, myself.

61

I could be Earl . . . I could be Earl, or Mason, or Titus, or Conroy . . . any of them . . . I got to analyze it out, if only I could have some quiet. But there is this racket, this commotion . . . bangin' on the ceiling and the walls an' yellin' down in the street . . . an' people up close to me, crowdin' an' yellin' like all my life . . . I got to sanctify the space around me

(*indicates space around his body*)

but I got to do it myself, it is a hard task . . . it is askin' a lot . . .

SCENE 10

The Skinner living room. MASON lying on the sofa.
MRS. SKINNER enters with KIDD.

MRS. S

Mr. Kidd, here is my son Mason. He very sharp, the sharpest
one— Mason, this is Mr. Kidd, that you' brother got retained for
the trial—he just wants to talk to you an' ask some things—

KIDD

Titus is certainly going to get free—there's no question about it.
He'll be acquitted. It's only a matter of the means we use to get
the acquittal—I want to use every possible means—

MASON

He goin' to request me to be a character witness, I know that,
well, I ain't goin' to make no public appearance in no
courtroom, that a final fact. Howcome that television off? I
watchin' the show—

(*sneering*)

Momma say I the sharpest one of the boys, she means I got the
good grades in school, which is a truth, but I turnin' my back on
that shit, an' I concentratin' on the television—I got nothin' to
say to you, Mr. Kidd.

KIDD

Mason, I only want to—

MASON

Howcome I *Mason* to you so fast?

MRS. S

Mason, you bein' damn rude!

KIDD

(*embarrassed, awkward; then cleverly*)

I think of you as Mason, because your brother speaks of you that way . . . and your mother, of course . . . and in my thoughts, when I think of you, I naturally think of *Mason*. But you're quite right, I shouldn't presume any intimacy with you. My own name is Harold—Harold Kidd. I only want to ask you a few questions—

MASON

(*his voice rising until it is shrill, mad*)

I say that I livin' here in my own skin which is me, my own possession, an' I say you ain't gon' burn or cut it off me . . . nobody gettin' through that doorway to do it . . . there is a skeleton inside gon' fight you like hell, for the true ownership of that skin . . . .

KIDD

(*to MRS. SKINNER*)

What's wrong? What's happened to him?

MRS. S

Mason, he just goin' through a phase—a bad phase of his life— He very excitable, he don't take them pills like the prescription says to—

MASON

I'm in charge of myself! I can handle myself! I'm in sovereign control!

KIDD

Mason, I only want to help you and your family—I don't want to upset you— Believe me, please, this isn't just a job to me, this case isn't just an ordinary case, it has deep, terrible symbolic value—it goes far beyond itself and into history—

MASON

Don't you come near me!

KIDD

But I only want—

(*BOB enters*)

MASON

These hands is not black or white or any color—these hands is on their own an' itchin' for somebody to rip—if somebody gets too close—

KIDD

Look, I know what you've gone through. I *know*. All your lives you people have been made to know that your birth, the color of your skin, is your fate—your skins are your fate—the shape of your lips is your *fate*— No one has ever looked at you, at your humanity— Do you think I don't know? Do you think all white men are blind to you?

MASON

I gon' skin you, hang it up on the door outside—I gon' defend myself inch by inch—outward mutilation if necessary—

BOB

(*shouting*)

Jesus, Mason, you goin' crazy! You crazy-mouth, crazy shit-head—

MASON

You an' him both stay away—I am warnin' you— Nobody's goin' get close to me again an' torture my face—I refuse it—I goin' defend every inch—

BOB

All this talk is just a way he got, a way he usin'—he wants Titus to get found guilty—he wants Titus to suffer—all this crazy-shit talk is just put-on . . . .

(*He goes to MASON, tries to pull him up. MASON resists.*)

All of us is goin' to talk for Titus—we goin' step up front at that courtroom—an' you goin' do you' share an' show you' goddam messed-up face—damn you—

MRS. S

Bob!

BOB

Momma, you to blame in this—you lettin' him lay here for a month—ain't had no bath, just lays there watchin' television— Momma, *he* ain't no worse off than anybody else—he just tryin' to die—

MRS. S

(*slaps him*)

Little show-off snot! You goin' make a good appearance for Titus, ain't you—showin' off right now? You think this is the trial, this is the courthouse?—you showin' off in front of Mr. Kidd here? Well, Mr. Kidd he got better sense than to give any goddam about you' opinions— Get out of here an' let Mason alone.

BOB

If he don't do the right thing for Titus—if he let Titus down I goin' kill him myself an' finish the job—

(*exits*)

MRS. S

Mr. Kidd, we goin' leave you two some privacy, to talk in peace. I sure am sorry for all this . . .

(*exits*)

(*KIDD, alone with MASON, looks at him, uneasily. For a while he doesn't speak. Nervously, he opens his briefcase and takes out some papers, leafs through them. MASON is lying back as if exhausted, one arm dangling down off the sofa. He is breathing hard.*)

KIDD

The trial is set now for October 11 . . . I tried to get it postponed again but I couldn't . . . but . . . but I'm confident we'll win . . . I'm confident . . . . But I need everyone's aid, I need character witnesses . . . I need someone as articulate as yourself and . . . and . . . as tragic . . . Mason? Can you hear me?

(*KIDD approaches MASON, slowly. MASON turns his head away, hardly an inch or so away, so that KIDD cannot meet his gaze. KIDD involuntarily touches his own face, gropingly, as if recoiling from MASON'S deformity.*)

Mason, no one is going to hurt you. No one. Ever again . . . My God, . . . is that painful? . . . your face . . . ?

(*When MASON does not reply, KIDD speaks more normally.*)

Well, look. I'll get those boys acquitted, right here at home, the jury will see through the prosecution's flimsy case—not *one* eyewitness!—a discredited confession!—I'll demolish the prosecution's main argument, and it will give me great joy to do so . . . Mason, you're listening, aren't you? Mason? I only want you to take the stand very briefly, to say just a few words on behalf of your brother . . . to explain, uh, what kind of a brother he was . . . did he buy things for you and your family, like, uh, things in this room . . . and did he show affection for . . .

(*MASON shudders and turns away, child-like.*)

. . . there's no risk involved. No risk. I know threats have been made against your family—even against me for defending your brother—but nothing will happen, no one will dare hurt us—

(*proudly*)

Threats have been made against me a half-dozen times in the past few years, but I haven't been intimidated. No one is going to intimidate *me*. Once I opened a package that came to me at my office—and it was a fake bomb—it was a cheap alarm clock tricked up to resemble a bomb—but a *fake* bomb, just to scare me—I was defending some conscientious objectors at the time— But the point is, the point is, the bomb was a *fake*—it was only meant to frighten me away— Most things are fakes when you examine them; they don't explode.

MASON

Leave me alone—

KIDD

No one is going to hurt you, Mason.

(*pause*)

The men who tortured you are dead.

MASON

(*looking around mockingly*)

Who's dead? Where are they dead?

KIDD

Your torturers are dead—they're both dead—

MASON

Both?

68

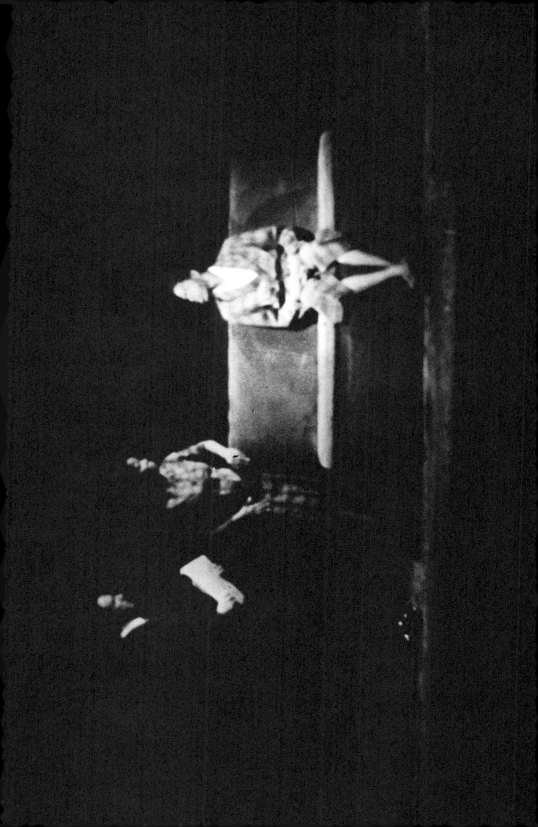

KIDD

Both men.

MASON

Both? Both means *two* . . . ?

KIDD

Yes, two. Two. They're both dead. They're *dead*.

MASON

Two? . . . There was a lot more than two of them . . . .

KIDD

What?

MASON

I don't believe it. I want proof. I am never leavin' this place without absolute proof. Mr. Kidd, the whole universe better be dead before I riskin' it.

KIDD

Mason, if only you—

MASON

Who this *Mason* you always addressin'? He some brother to you, or somethin'? You know him by sight—or what? What's he look like, you so close to him?—you so easy with him?

KIDD

I'm sorry, I'm sorry if I—I'll call you Mr. Skinner—I—

MASON

Which one are you?

(confused)

I don't see the right way now . . . all the stuff is blurred, it all crooked an' sideways . . . . Howcome you in here, in my Momma's house?

KIDD

(*frightened*)

Mason, my name is Harold Kidd . . . I'm your brother's attorney . . .

(*After an awkward pause, KIDD walks away and begins a kind of speech, pacing around the room, excitedly, passionately; alternated with his speech is MASON'S speech, which is delivered as he lies immobile.*)

. . . my purpose is victory, another victory . . . another in a sequence of hard-fought hard-won victories . . . to be headlined everywhere, in all the newspapers . . . shouted everywhere in all the small towns . . . under the paving stones of the country . . . A victory for your race, for the new dawn of this nation . . . for freedom, for justice, for *you* . . .

MASON

This place of my Momma's not secret enough to keep noises away. You got to burrow under the wallpaper to get safe. Or else they come trampin' in here—too many people—they turn off the television set an' start their own kind of television show an' the noise of it makes me awful nervous. When I get my own strength back, I goin' burrow under the wallpaper an' plaster an' stuff to find some peace.

KIDD

. . . I have a vision in which the Potomac overflows its banks . . . and everything is mud, dense black evil mud, choking, suffocating everyone in its path . . . black mud like lava . . . a great mass without individual parts, without souls or faces . . . just an avalanche of mud . . . there will be no need for fire, for explosions . . . the mud will take everything before it . . . and . . . and the rest of us . . . men like myself . . . men with brains and maps of the future . . . the rest of us will wait joyfully, we will guide and instruct and navigate the future . . . . Men have always been one-dimensional, except the men who write the history books! I plan on writing a book of my own, *my own*. I know what I'm doing. I can get the mud-flow started because . . . I don't think it's really going to happen . . . I mean, not *really* . . . . It couldn't really happen . . . .

(KIDD pauses, glances at MASON, who ignores him. He starts to leave, and BOB stops him in the hallway.)

BOB

Hey—Mr. Kidd—you talked any sense in him?

KIDD

I'm absolutely confident—yes—I'm confident that your brother will come around to our way of thinking. We've been talking about many important things . . . the need for cooperation, for a united front . . . I'm confident it will turn out well.

BOB

You sure . . . ? He goin' to be acquitted, you *sure*?

KIDD

Yesterday afternoon the defense committee received a check for $100,000. History is being made.

BOB

Uh . . . $100,000? Who gave you that much money?

KIDD

Gentle people, people who wish to remain anonymous, men of my race who are fierce that justice be done . . . .

BOB

But who are they?

KIDD

Friends of yours. Friends of your brother's. Serious alarmed gentle people in this city . . . .

BOB

Hey, I mean, who got $100,000 to give away? I mean . . . uh . . . howcome they got so much, to hand out like that?

(KIDD exits; BOB calls after him.)

Mr. Kidd? Hey, if I had what it takes to give away $100,000, I would give it away too . . . only I ain't got that much . . . only I am real happy an' thankful an' so is Titus, I speak for Titus here, an' all the rest of us . . . only I got this simple question: howcome there is somebody got so much he can give that much away . . . ?

SCENE 11

Courtroom. BEATIE is being examined by the PROSECUTOR. On her right, at his raised bench is the JUDGE; to her left, the jury box, with twelve white jurors seated in it, these men and women out of the light, dimly-seen. On the other side of the stage is the defense counsel's table, at which TITUS, and KIDD sit; they too are out of the light.

BEATIE

. . . Yes, that is right. Yes. Then he said to me, like he said a whole lot of times, he said, *Anytime anybody cross me, I got the where-abouts to take care of him.*

PROSECUTOR

Did Titus Skinner ever mention to you, or boast to you, that he had punished anyone in the past?

BEATIE

Yes, yes, that is right . . . Yes. Yes, he did . . . .

(growing frightened)

Yes, I heard that. I heard something like that.

PROSECUTOR

Is it a fact that on the night of April 3 you were in the company of Titus Skinner?

BEATIE

(*slowly*)

Yes . . . that was a day . . . that was a date . . . .

PROSECUTOR

Would you speak more clearly, please, Miss Roscoe?

BEATIE

I think . . . yes . . . I think that was a date I remember, that something happened on . . . .

PROSECUTOR

On the night of April 3, how would you describe Titus Skinner's behavior to you?

BEATIE

He . . . he said . . . . He . . . .

(*A change comes over BEATIE; she begins to speak in fragments, in a tortuous manner, as if something were preventing her from speaking clearly. She is baffled, struggling to speak, but unable.*)

BEATIE

. . . then he said . . . he wanted

(*after a pause*)

I don't remember.

PROSECUTOR

(*stunned*)

I beg your pardon?

BEATIE

I don't remember.

74

(Everyone on stage shows some surprise; even the JUDGE glances down at BEATIE, for the first time.)

PROSECUTOR

Miss Roscoe, I beg your pardon . . . ? Were you answering my question . . . ? I'll read you my question again and . . . .

BEATIE

No, I don't remember. I don't think so. No. I don't think I was there.

PROSECUTOR

But Miss Roscoe, you were explaining to the court how, on the night of April 3, Titus Skinner took you to his room on West 119th Street, and—and you took from him, did you not, you took from him a quantity of heroin in a—

KIDD

Objection!

(SOUND: gavel)

PROSECUTOR

(very upset, awkward; glances out at the audience, embarrassed)

I seem to be . . . I . . . . Your Honor, my witness is not well . . . .

BEATIE

(girlishly)

I am fine, I am in fine spirits! I am feelin' very fine!

PROSECUTOR

(trying to resume his normal manner)

Miss Roscoe, will you go over the events of the night of April 3, please, to the best of your ability . . . ?

75

BEATIE

What April 3? When? I don't remember it, I wasn't there. I don't know who it was there with him—he brought a girl back with him, yes, he was always hangin' on some girl— A big handsome son of a bitch—Titus Skinner—if that's who you are referring to—

(*shocked; pretends to be surprised at her own words, looking around courtroom, then over at TITUS.*)

Jesus, I got to watch my mouth! I got a bad troublemakin' mouth!

(*makes an effort to be serious, in a school-girlish manner*)

But the fact is, you people that are listenin', I hope you are fully listenin', out there, the fact is this: a man got to trounce on a woman, an' if she hangs on him she's saying to him O.K. She's givin' to him that privilege. If she don't prefer that treatment she don't hang on him . . . . My Momma instructed me, she said, Beatie, if you drop out of that school—it was the LaMarvel Beauty College—if you violate that fifty-dollar tuition, then the hell with you, an' you better move right in with you' fancy boy friend, 'cause I ain't havin' none of you. She made it clear enough. But. But I got my head all wild, the more I told them friends of mine an' the girls at the school how I was drivin' all over town with Titus Skinner, the more I talked the wilder I got, just in my head, and Jesus I got high on him!—so I thought why the hell keep down so low, just to learn how to shampoo people's heads that is too freaky lazy to do it themselves, an' white ladies givin' me dime tips, an' all that shit you got to take from a boss—why—then I was crossin' right over to a new life, an' Titus Skinner standin' there on the curb, waitin'. So. So, that happened that way . . . So I made a cross-over, I made the decision. So I got no lies to spread about him, I got no complaints. He had lots of girls hangin' on him an' I pushed the other ones out, so he got the right to do what he cares to, an' I ain't in no position as it appears to make testimony against him . . . .

76

PROSECUTOR

(*angrily*)

Your Honor, my witness has obviously been intimidated—the court should know that her brother Conroy was found dead last night in—

KIDD

Objection! Your Honor, the prosecution is—

(*SOUND: gavel*)

PROSECUTOR

(*frustrated*)

This is so obvious!

(*PROSECUTOR sits*)

BEATIE

What's obvious? Nothing is obvious!

KIDD

(*buoyant; approaching her happily*)

Miss Roscoe, you have described Titus Skinner as your "boy friend," have you not?

BEATIE

Yes. I mean . . . I was with him for a while, but there were other girls . . . like me . . . other girls like me . . . the same age . . . an' . . . an' . . .

(*laughs*)

. . . lookin' like me.

KIDD

And you are the sister of the murdered boy, Earl Roscoe, are you not?

BEATIE

That was his name. Yes. I think so, yes.

KIDD

How would you characterize your relationship with Mr. Skinner?

BEATIE

. . . what was that word . . . ? I, uh, I mixed-up . . . .

KIDD

Was Titus ever violent toward you?

BEATIE

Oh no.

KIDD

Was he kind to you—bought you presents, bought your mother something for her birthday?

BEATIE

(naively pleased)

Oh, you know about that? Yeah, Titus showed up with some crazy-big plant, some kind of complicated name to them, uh, with tinfoil an' a green ribbon wrapped around . . . uh . . . the flowers was dyed bright pink . . . an' my Momma was still in bed an' . . . . Jesus, she was so surprised! But how do you know about it . . . ?

(shaking her head)

That Titus, he always done things to his own style!

KIDD

So the defendent was kind to you? Was he gentle to you, was he
loving to you . . . ?

BEATIE

Oh yes. Yes.

KIDD

Titus Skinner suffers from a bad reputation, would you say? a
misleading reputation?

BEATIE

Oh Jesus yes. Yes. He just too big for the neighborhood an' the
neighborhood tryin' to pull him down.

KIDD

The neighborhood, the people on the street, created a rumor to
the effect that Titus Skinner and his friends were responsible for
the murder of your brother and—

BEATIE

(*interrupting his last several words, as if not wanting to
hear them*)

Oh yeah! yeah! It was just nigger-talk . . . all kinds of jealous
mother-fuckers, shootin' their damn mouths off . . . . On
account of, you know,

(*earnestly, to audience*)

there is a low-lyin' mediocre element in the world, anxious to
pull down big men . . . got to tear their wings off at the shoulders
. . . Now Titus, what he needed was, maybe, was, uh, he was
like one of them famous generals only he was hid-away
somewhere, like on a farm out in the country, feedin' the cows or
whatever they got on a farm . . . and, uh, somebody come ridin'
along on a horse an' told the news about a big invasion . . . an'
the general, who was only a man feedin' cows at the time, why,
he thrown all that shit down an' walked right out there an'

walked right into the picture books . . . . Only, only Titus never got that kind of news brought to him: so he kind of, you know, kind of had to invent the way out for himself . . . .

KIDD

Then in your intimate knowledge of Titus Skinner's character, Miss Roscoe, in your very intimate and yet objective assessment of the likelihood of his—of his being involved—in the crime of which he is accused, you would say—you would say—?

BEATIE

It's hands-off him. You better let him loose.

KIDD

You haven't been intimidated, Miss Roscoe, have you?

BEATIE

(*staring*)

. . . huh?

KIDD

Recent, uh, developments . . . and the atmosphere of the case . . . haven't intimidated you, have they? You haven't been approached, I mean, by anyone, and threatened . . . ?

(*When BEATIE seems not to comprehend, he speaks simply and loudly, as if to a child.*)

You haven't been coerced in any way, have you, Miss Roscoe?

BEATIE

(*after a long pause*)

Coerced . . . ? Coerced?

*(The rest of the stage darkens again; the spotlight is on
BEATIE, but mellow.)*

Coerced . . . ? What word is that . . . ?

SCENE 12

The courtroom.

TITUS

Howcome my attorney didn't want me to stop up here, I don't know . . . he needs more faith in me . . . he's too nervous . . . I said to him *All them other people goin' to talk about me, an' I ain't goin' to be allowed up there?—ain't goin' to be allowed the final word?* Jesus, that looked to me like a sure give-away, that I had something to hide, an' any jury at all, if they are all white people like this jury, or all black, or in-between, they are not goin' to take the correct impression out of that. My attorney said it was a strategy, his way, but I told him I determined the strategy of my own life. I always have done that, an' I always turned out O.K. . . . Most of the time.

(*TITUS steps down from the witness stand, walks out onto the stage. He glances down at himself, checking his appearance, clears his throat, shows some signs of nervousness, but also eagerness, pleasure. It is obvious that he enjoys himself—his voice, his behavior, his being—and there is a kind of close, intimate awareness of his "being," which most of the other people in the play, especially Conroy and Mason and Beatie, do not exhibit; as if they were somehow strangers to themselves, trying to figure out what their relationship is to these strangers. TITUS, most of all, is not a "healthy animal" but a healthy-seeming human being—the animalistic quality is important, he is physically impressive, strong, tall, etc., but it is subordinate to his more conscious awareness of himself. Yet he is not*

83

"heroic"—he must be played as a murderer.)

TITUS

A few years ago I had a dream . . .

(*clearing his throat; louder*)

A few years ago I had a dream . . . I mean a dream like at night
. . . an' I don't have dreams like other people, almost never, I
just fall into bed an' sleep hard, an' wake up all ready for the
next day. But I had a dream, this dream

(*indicates the scene around him*)

that I was on trial . . . on trial for something I did or didn't do,
. or something somebody did, somewhere along the line . . . uh . . .
an' damn if it don't all come back to me! I mean, I prophesized
all this shit!—the talk, an' the way it looks here, people sittin'
around gawkin' at me—rows an' rows of people starin' an'
listenin'—damn if it wasn't a crazy dream, lookin' back on it,
like you do with dreams that turn out to be true! . . . This dream
come to me years ago, when I was just a skinny scrawny little
kid, with no pride to me except what was layin' in wait, in my
head.

(*He touches his head, his face, as if presenting it to the
audience; his manner is kingly, he considers himself
worthy of display.*)

I prophesized this scene for myself. It was Titus Skinner not yet
thirty years old, on trial for murder in this city, in a courtroom
that looked like this. Jesus, I had a real dream of it! And I woke
up sweating and scared as hell an' I said to myself *Titus, better
get the hell out of this city—you headin' for real trouble!* But, to
keep a balance, I also said *Titus, there is risks necessary for any
man.* So I hung around an' here I am today . . . . The dream had
a judge, a white man like him, an', uh, lots of white people
around . . . like the men askin' all the questions, one side an' then
the other, my side an' then their side, all white men askin'
questions an' presentin' a case, the way they do, according to
their *strategy*.

84

(mockingly)

Which is the white man's strategy, like my attorney tried to say,
keeping me from my own defense . . . it's courtroom strategy, so
he told me, but hell with that. So this is the outcome of the
dream: I in a bad spot, I sweatin' like a pig inside my new
clothes, an' I really, uh, I really in for some trouble now,
because they is all catchin' up with me an' tryin' to show how I
did some crime, that is provable an' against the law. Jesus, how
you like that?—that's a tight spot! So to get out of it I did some
magic, real magic, like a trick of a magician, you know, that I
never even thought about in real life, when I was awake, an'
everything turned out O.K. That is the hell of it! The surprise of
it! . . . One time my brother Mason, that is messed up now in the
face an' in the head, an' who is right now layin' on the sofa in my
Momma's living room, where he goin' to lay the rest of his
life . . . my brother Mason, when he was a little kid, memorized
a poem for school an' went around the house recitin' it, an' he
got it down just perfect an' on the right day he went to school an'
damn if he didn't say it out just perfect . . .

(shakes his head)

Only time he ever done anything to impress me! The poem never
made no sense to me, but it went along O.K. an' sounded O.K.
Mason never done anything before or since that day. But
anyway he done *that* . . . . In my dream I perform a trick of
magic, an' everybody so damn impressed they clap their hands
an' say to the jail-people *Let Titus Skinner go free!* The people
clap their hands though they hate me like hell, they *really* hate
me, but, shit, they got to admit in their heads that I am high-
level to bring off the trick, an' it in the fair play, you know, the
interests of open market, that I got to be rewarded.

(looks around, gets silent assent)

So I will do that trick now an' see what happens . . . .

*(As if this isn't well-planned, he looks around and the
court clerk, a servile white man, steps hesitantly
forward, confers with TITUS briefly, glances back at
the JUDGE, hurries off-stage to reappear with a large*

light bulb and some wire, looped around his arm.
TITUS gives him instructions, and while the clerk
winds one end of the wire around TITUS'S ankle,
TITUS wipes his forehead, turned halfway to the
audience. He is excited, keyed-up, nervous. The clerk
unwinds the wire until he is nearly out of sight in the
darkness at the rear of the stage.)

TITUS

You got that plugged in?—is there a socket back there?

(*to audience*)

He pluggin' that in. All this is a wire for electricity, here. See, it's
got the insulation, or whatever they call it. And this-here is a
100-watt bulb, it says so on the top of it . . . all this small part's
too trivial for my dream, the dream took care of itself an' didn't
bother with such nuisance. O.K., you got that plugged in? Now
I will explain: every black boy in America has a certain thought,
that he grows up into, an' that is the electric chair . . . but damn
if they ain't gettin' rid of it, state by state . . . an' I expect it will
turn up like the wild animals in a museum somewhere, where
you can't get at it. That changes a way of life. That modifies a
way of life. But I was born at such a time that I had a long
expectation of it, the electric chair, an' it made me think fast, an'
I come to like it, you know, in a crazy way . . . how you get to
like something you been adjacent to for awhile . . . .

(*boastfully*)

In fact, you people are comin' to like *me* . . . I *very* adjacent to
you. However, this is the fact: that the trick of the electric-stuff
is in my head, like in all black boys' heads, an' their mommas
naturally got that worry also, so it a family enterprise. But I am
not a nigger, I am something else, an' that allow me to triumph
over the shitty little trick of the electric-magic, which is just some
plugged-in strategy, that anybody could do if he pulled the
switch . . . . So I take this 100-watt bulb an' I display it like this

(*holds it high, in his right hand; like a sword or a*
torch)

an' I talk to myself in utter confidence . . . in the magic, that it will work. You watch.

(He closes his eyes, holds one hand to his forehead as if concentrating very hard.)

. . . Here is the need for some hard concentration!

(He tries again, seems to be straining, so that his face twists into a mask of anguish.)

This calls for strong energies . . . all the flow-through of the energies that is loose in here, an' in the universe . . . but I equal to it, I an't goin' to back away . . . .

(Finally, the light bulb actually lights up. TITUS holds it proudly aloft. He makes a slight, mocking bow to the audience and to the people on stage with him, who applaud his trick falteringly—some of them not clapping, only staring in horror; others clapping briskly but hollowly. TITUS bows again to the real audience, as the stage lights dim slowly until only his light remains; then that is extinguished.)

Printed October 1974 in Santa Barbara & Ann Arbor for the
Black Sparrow Press by Noel Young & Edwards Brothers Inc.
Design by Barbara Martin. This edition is published in paper
wrappers; there are 1000 hardcover copies; & 350 copies
handbound in boards by Earle Gray numbered & signed by the
author.

Photo: Raymond Smith

From the start of her writing career, Joyce Carol Oates has earned high literary acclaim. She was awarded a Guggenheim Fellowship in 1967-1968 and the Richard and Hinda Rosenthal Foundation Award for her novel *A Garden of Earthly Delights* (1967). Her novel, *them*, won the National Book Award for Fiction in 1970. *The Wheel of Love* (1970) contains many prize-winning stories. Black Sparrow Press published *The Hungry Ghosts: Seven Allusive Comedies* in the spring of 1974, and in the spring of 1975 will publish *The Seduction & Other Stories*.